P9-CDP-096

Containing some account of its Geology, Geography and Anthropology, its influence on the people of its valley, and their use of it.

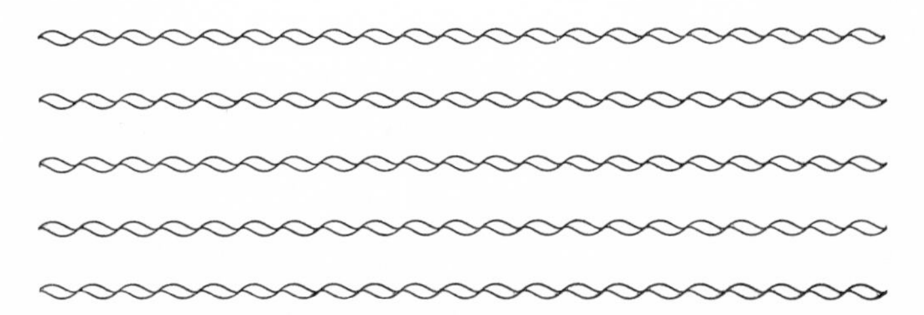

Barre Publishers, Barre, Massachusetts

1964

For Colby Junior College

Laurence Eaton Richardson

Concord River

by

Laurence Eaton Richardson

with the photographs of

Katharine Knowles

" . . . My house stands in low land, with limited outlook, and on the skirt of the village. But I go with my friend to the shore of our little river, and with one stroke of the paddle I leave the village politics and personalities, yes, and the world of villages and personalities behind, and pass into a delicate realm of sunset and moonlight, too bright almost for spotted man to enter without novitiate and probity. We penetrate bodily this incredible beauty: we dip our hands in this painted element: our eyes are bathed in these lights and forms . . . "

from the essay "NATURE" by R. W. Emerson

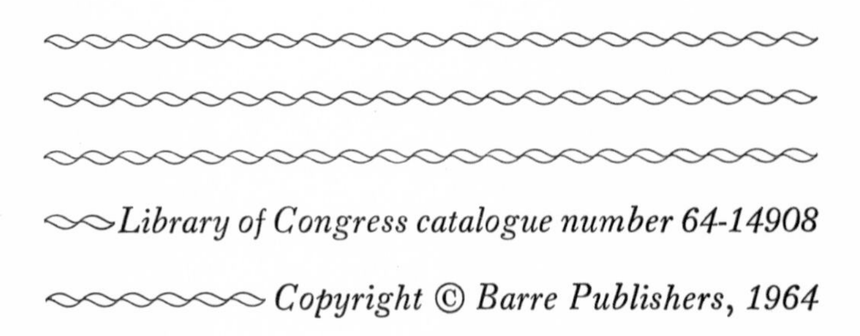

Library of Congress catalogue number 64-14908

*W**ITHIN* the last few years, the people of this valley have come to realize that they are in danger of losing the river as they know it. Fortunately a few worthy people have worked hard to forestall this loss and see that as much as possible of this priceless asset to our rural, or at least suburban residential surroundings is saved. We, in Concord, think of the river as the winding stretch of water, eleven miles up to Wayland and eleven down to Billerica, all with generally the same characteristics of a narrow nearly stagnant stream through broad meadows most of the year, but rising sometimes more than once to cover the meadows with an expanse of water, in some places nearly a mile wide. This stream first called Musketaquid, then the Great River, then the Concord, even up in Hopkinton, was later the Hopkinton above Framingham, the Sudbury below in Sudbury, and finally a little over a hundred years ago, the map-makers called the whole south branch the Sudbury; the north branch the Assabet, and the river below their junction, the Concord.

Whatever its name, it is the river Emerson spoke of in his poems and essays, Thoreau and Hawthorne in their books, and Brewster in his diary of which one published volume of selections is entitled "Concord River". We recognize it from Hawthorne's "Notes". "This river of ours is the most sluggish stream that I ever was acquainted with . . . Owing to this torpor of the stream, it has nowhere a bright, pebbly shore, nor is there so much as a narrow strip of glistening sand in any part of its course; but it slumbers along between broad meadows, or kisses the tangled grass of mowing-fields and pastures, or bathes the overhanging boughs of elder bushes and other water loving plants . . . . I bathe, once, and often twice, a day in our river; but one dip into the salt sea would be worth more than a whole week's soaking in such a lifeless tide . . . . Its hue has a slight tinge of gold, and my limbs, when I behold them through its medium, look tawny . . . . But taking the river all in all, I can find nothing more fit to compare it with than one of the half-torpid earthworms that I dig up for bait. The worm is sluggish, and so is the river, — the river is muddy and so is the worm. You hardly know whether either of them be alive or dead; but still in the course of time, they both manage to creep away."

Many other writers have described the appearance of the river in Concord; but where does it come from? where does it go? how has it influenced the people who have lived near it? how have they used and abused it? what is it like over its whole extent? Only with answers to these questions can we really know and understand it. To broaden your image of the Concord River, think of it not as the river of Thoreau or the Flood arched by the rude bridge, but the river which flows from the birthplace of Eli Whitney in Westborough to that of James Abbott McNeill Whistler in Lowell, and has turned the wheels of over 50 different mills at one time or another, ranging in size from the one horse grist-mill of Colonial days to the largest woolen mill in the world during the early part of this century. This was at Maynard on the Assabet, and needs to be mentioned to emphasize the fact that though hiding in woods and narrow valleys, it is larger than the Sudbury or South Branch which is exposed in its wide meadows for all to see.

The Assabet has always been overlooked from the time William Wood, the first white man to see the Concord River, followed its course up from the Merrimack, and viewed Nashawtuc Hill from the ridge east of Monument Street when the meadows were flooded, and concluded it was an island. When he went back to London and published his book "New England's Prospects" in 1632, he included a map showing the Concord and Sudbury Rivers which together he called the Musketaquid, with the Assabet circling around the hill and joining the Sudbury again at what was to be the Stone Bridge on Elm Street. Compare what Hawthorne said of the Concord and Sudbury with his description of the Assabet in "Mosses from an Old Manse". "Rowing our boat against the current, between wide meadows, we turn aside into the Assabeth. A more lovely stream than this, for a mile above its junction with the Concord, has never flowed on earth, — nowhere, indeed, except to lave the interior of a poet's imagination. It is sheltered from the breeze by woods and a hillside; so that elsewhere there might be a hurricane, and here scarcely a ripple across the shaded water . . . . It comes flowing softly through the midmost privacy and deepest heart of a wood which whispers back again from its sedgy borders, as if the river and wood were hushing one another to sleep." But the Assabet is, as stated, a larger part than the Sudbury in the total flow of the Concord.

The larger brooks, too, that contribute to all three sections of the river must be considered in any survey of the valley, and a geographical description may well be given here now, to include all the territory on which rain or snow falling, ultimately ends up in the Concord River when it empties into the Merrimack. This valley is much greater than you would think. The watershed as it would be called is somewhat fan-shaped and extends over about 400 square miles. Thirty-six towns lie wholly or partly within it. Both the Assabet and the Sudbury came from swamps which lie near the main line of the Boston & Albany Railroad in the town of Westborough, the Assabet from the west side, near the Grafton State Hospital, and the Sudbury from the south, due east of the center of Westborough. Substantial brooks flow into each of these swamps, however, so the real sources (those most distant) are in the case of the Assabet, brooks in Grafton; and in the case of the Sudbury, brooks in Upton.

From Westborough the Assabet takes a fairly straight north-east course through Northborough, the corner of Marlborough, Hudson, Stow, Maynard, and just a corner of Acton into Concord where it meets the Sudbury, which from Westborough has flowed due east along the southern border of Southborough through Ashland to Framingham, and then north dividing Wayland from Sudbury, much of the way, and then Lincoln from Concord until reaching Fairhaven Bay after which it is all through Concord to the meeting with the Assabet. From this point, the Concord flows generally north-east until it turns north where it forms the boundary between Concord and Bedford, then between Bedford and Carlisle into Billerica. From here it bounds Chelmsford for about a mile, and touches Tewksbury to enter Lowell and its confluence with the Merrimack. Towns largely drained by tributary brooks and not mentioned as one of those through which one of the rivers flow are

Hopkinton, Berlin, Bolton, and extensive areas of Sherburne, Natick, Shrewsbury, Boylston, Harvard, Boxborough, Littleton and Westford. Thus it is evident that the river spreads its influence over a large area.

With this picture in mind, let us go back a long way into the past and tell something of the conditions over the years up to the present time, starting at the beginning of the retreat of the last glacier of those that overran the land intermittently for perhaps one million years. This is estimated to have begun about 15,000 years ago. When the last glacier was at its most southern point, extending to the vicinity of Narragansett Bay, hundreds, maybe thousands of feet of ice covered our river valleys. Approaching 10,000 B. C. however, the climate moderated and a final gradual retreat of the ice sheet began. This was not steady but the average over the years amounted to about 100 feet a year or nearly two miles a century. It was a long time before the southern edge of the ice got north into our valley and those adjacent, but finally it did, melting on top, rotting, breaking into pieces and depositing its burden of rocks, sand, and gravel, making the topography somewhat as we see it to-day. Due to the release of the weight of the ice, the land to the south may have risen, but at any rate the melting glacial waters and the seasonal rains could not flow north because of the ice, and large lakes were formed which overflowed eastward. The lake in the Nashua River valley flowed across into the Sudbury, and this in turn emptied into the lower Charles River basin and thus to the ocean. What is known to geologists as Glacial Lake Sudbury extended from Framingham to Concord, about twenty miles long and about four wide. It spilled over into the Charles at three different places at different times as the ice dams melted; first through the gap at Sandy Pond in Lincoln into Hobbs Brook, now flooded for the Cambridge Water Supply, later through the Cherry Brook valley into Weston, and finally through the low land near Cochituate into Lake Waban. All the ice did not melt at one time in a given area. Floating bergs stranded and became covered with sediment and remained for years to make the so-called pot-holes when they finally melted which we see scattered over our country-side, and the greater hollows, now filled with water such as Walden and White Pond in Concord. Long tongues of ice also stuck out from the front of the glacier deflecting the running water so that the sediment it carried was deposited in the various forms that we still see as ridges, and making long swamps when they finally melted. It was during this time too that the water which flowed into the lake gave up its burden of clay and sand to make the wide plains at different levels that are so much a part of our valley picture to-day.

Eventually the ice retreated freeing the Merrimack, and the rivers taking up their natural channels turned north and began to cut their way through the debris that the glacier had left behind. Occasionally floating ice still obstructed the free flow of the stream, as for example, a large block which damned the Assabet in Concord above the Elm Street bridge causing the water to turn down to join the Sudbury through the gap between the railroad and Main Street.

The rivers when they turned north had little difficulty cutting through the glacial till to the high places in the bed rock beneath, and upstream from each of these the cutting ceased as the current slackened, but below, the rushing waters continued on until held up by another. The character of the rivers has been determined by these ledges, and their location accounts for some of the difference between the Sudbury and Assabet. They start out much alike, the brooks at the headwaters of each originate at altitudes of four or five hundred feet, and as said before flow into swamps one or two hundred feet below, with an altitude in the case of Cedar Swamp where the Sudbury starts, of 274 feet and the Assabet swamp 300 feet, or 26 feet higher. From these swamps down, the rivers started making their channels. The Sudbury had an easy time. In twelve miles it descends 160 feet to below Saxonville after which it barely flows the ten miles to its juncture with the Assabet. The Assabet, however, takes 18 miles to drop 160 feet, which it has done below Maynard, and it still has 26 feet more to go to its meeting with the Sudbury six miles away. After the two branches join in the Concord, there is hardly any drop over the ten miles to the Fordway bar in North Billerica. From this point there is a total drop of about fifty feet over several ledges in the final six miles to the Merrimack.

Following the glacial retreat came plants from the south. Animals followed the plants and man followed the animals. Soon after 2000 B.C. we know men lived in this vicinity because when the subway was being dug near the corner of Clarendon Street and Boylston, in Boston, a fish weir was found and examined by archeologists of nearby universities. The Back Bay had been filled in but the weir was found below the former natural level and it was confidently stated that at the time of its use the water in the Atlantic Ocean was some thirteen feet lower than it is to-day, presumably because a large amount was frozen up in the glaciers to the north. The first people to live here in this valley were hunters and fishermen, thought by some to be represented in archeological records as the Red Paint people whose graves have been found in Northern New England, and who may have been last known in a disappearing tribe described by early voyagers to Newfoundland. They probably got pushed north as our climate was getting warmer by people known as Algonquin who came from the southwest, and whose culture is known from the contents of the mounds they built in Ohio. The Algonquins came bringing their corn, beans, pumpkins and tobacco, for the climate had become very warm, much warmer than to-day, reaching a climax about 1200 B. C. At some point the tribes then in New England were cut off from their main body by the Iroquois in New York, and as the climate cooled and they could not always rely on their tender vegetables and corn, they learned to supplement their agriculture with meat and fish, nuts, berries, acorns, fruit and other products of the fields and forest. The valley was able to satisfy the requirements for their existence. The unforested river meadows and level plains could be burned over to provide fields for their crops, and attractive pastures for deer and other animals which they would snare or capture with spears and arrows; and the river itself provided fish.

For these early people, the river was a natural avenue for transportation and communication. Gookin, writing about these Indians in the early part of the seventeenth century, describes the method: "For their water passage, travels and fishing, they make boats or canoes, either of great trees, made hollow and artificially; which they do by burning them; and after with scraping, smoothly shaping them. Of these they make greater or lesser. Some *I have* seen will carry 20 persons, being 40-50 feet in length. They make another sort of conoes of birchen bark". Probably there was not enough of the large paper birch locally to make the large canoes, but smaller ones were made of laminated bark bent around a simple framework of any well seasoned hardwood, bound and held by fibrous roots and animal sinews, and made waterproof by a compound of grease and pitch. These small canoes were very light and could easily be carried by one man from river to river or lake when the route so required.

There is plenty of evidence showing the occupation of the valley. The sites of the villages of the subtribe, the Nipmucks, of the Massachusetts Indians, have been found at almost every suitable spot along the local rivers, always on elevations or knolls, to be above the spring floods. Over 25,000 specimens of their stone weapons or implements have been found in Concord alone, from sites located along the river at Ball's Hill and opposite, below Punkatasset and across by the town filter beds, at Hildreth's corner, near Spencer Brook north of Barrett's Mill Road, north of Warner's Pond near Route 2, near Simon Willard Road, around Mt. Misery at Fairhaven Bay, and both sides of the river at Pantry Brook. Farther up the river there was among other places a large site at Heard Pond in Wayland and the falls at Saxonville was crowded during the fishing season. The big fishing spot, however, was near the mouth of the river at Wamesit (now Lowell) and Gookin reports that he saw an estimated 12,000 Indians congregated there during the three weeks in the spring when the fish were running.

The Indians moved frequently from one site to another to be where food was most easily available. As at Wamesit, when the fish began to run up the streams in the spring they would set weirs across the narrower rapids, to entangle the fish or so impede their progress that they could easily be speared or shot with arrows. Sometimes, even, the natural flow of the rapids or falls would cause the fish to pile up so that they could be scraped out with the hands. Besides food to be eaten, fish provided fertilizer for the crops. Bradford writes that Squanto told the Pilgrims "except they got fish and set with it, it (corn) would come to nothing."

After fishing, planting their fields was the other spring job, but then they made their annual summer move to the ocean. This for our Indians was a canoe trip down to the Merrimack and thence to the island bays and beaches near its mouth. Once at the ocean the food problem was solved for several months, and quantities of clams, lobster, and fish were dried for the winter months and carried back up river late in the summer. Then the crops were harvested and stored, the woods and fields burned over, and the pursuit of animals for meat and clothing was begun. Thus by winter a store had been laid by to feed everyone until another spring.

Besides the seasonal migrations, the natives used the river as a trade route to obtain desirable raw materials that were not available locally. These included the most easily worked slate or flint for knives, chisels, arrows or spear heads, soapstone for vessels, perhaps birch bark for the larger canoes, and iron pyrites for kindling fire. The north and south course of the river leading to the greater highway of the Merrimack made it a well used water pathway. The Nashua River to the west must have been similarly used but was not so available to tributary travel from the Boston basin up the Charles, or from Narragansett Bay up the Blackstone, for the headwaters of each of these was in Hopkinton near the start of a large brook flowing into the Sudbury. At various places in that and other nearby towns, the direction of the wind determined sometimes whether a drop of rain would end up in Boston Harbor, Narragansett Bay, or the Merrimack. Another link in the traffic pattern was the principal foot trail east and west which crossed the valley at Framingham, much as the present turnpikes do to-day.

When the first English settlers came the Indians had had contact during their summer coastal life with European fishermen for more than a century and their culture had been affected to a considerable extent. They had acquired copper and brass in greater quantity than it had been previously available; also cloth and some other manufactured articles. Through this contact they got the plague, in 1617, which literally decimated their number, followed by small-pox a few years later and this greatly affected the history of the valley for there remained only a few hundred Indians in this valley when the first towns, Concord (1635), Sudbury (1639), Billerica and Chelmsford (1655), and Marlborough (1656) were settled. Therefore the English did not get to learn much of the Indian way of living.

But the fact that the Indians had been living here for centuries did help the colonists. When William Wood returned to Boston from his explorations and reported to his associates of which Simon Willard was one, he called attention to the meadows and cultivated fields along the rivers and pointed out the lack of competition from the few remaining Indians. He must surely have told them about the place called Musketaquid. Consequently when suitable farm land was getting scarce along the coast, Concord was the first inland settlement attempted; and within twenty-five years, Sudbury on the river above, Billerica and Chelmsford below, and Marlborough on the Assabet were occupied. These towns were contiguous, and except for Stow, settled a few years later, accountd for all the land along the rivers, which is now divided among many more. For example, Westborough, Southborough, Northborough and Hudson have all come out of Marlborough.

Thousands come to Concord each year
to see its bridge, its battleground and its river.

A pilgrim takes the walk across the bridge approaching the Minuteman Monument.

Concord Bridge.

America's most familiar monument.

From the North Bridge, a residence sits high above the bank.

Concord River below the North Bridge.

Summer clouds are reflected in the quiet waters of the Sudbury River.

Elm Street Bridge over the Sudbury River at Concord.

A view along the banks of the Sudbury.

A canoeist explores along the Assabet.

A memorial to George Ripley Bartlett, poet, journalist and beloved leader of late 19th century social life on the river, marks a boulder on the Assabet and, opposite, town historian Walcott's verse commemorating the Indian owners of Musketaquid stands at the meeting of the Sudbury and Assabet Rivers.

A summer morning at Concord Academy's boat landing.

Concord Academy Chapel from the River.

At Concord the Assabet flows quietly beneath the trees.

The Gate House at Damondale Mills in Concord stands on the site of one of the River's earliest cotton and woolen mills.

The Powder Mill Dam at Acton recalls an early New England industry.

A granite aqueduct crosses the Assabet at Northborough.

THE *ENGLISH* settlers cultivated the same fields, caught the same fish, and hunted the same animals, but they had a lot to learn before they had plenty, and there was disappointment. Almost at once, as early as 1636, the river, as it does to-day, got out of its banks, and the meadows were found to be much wetter than expected, and therefore of less usefulness. It was thought that obstructions down stream could be removed to relieve the condition and the General Court was petitioned by the inhabitants of Concord to provide that any drainage improvements which they made could be proportionally charged to other towns which might benefit, subsequently settled above them on the river. Again, in 1644, the Court took notice of the situation, and appointed commissioners "to set some order which may conduce to the better improving of the meadow, and saving and preserving of the hay there gotten . . . by draining the same . . . " This flooding continued and petitions were filed about every twenty years thereafter to get the government, colonial or state, to do something to help.

One advantage the settlers had, however, was the knowledge of how to use the water power available. Mostly they harnessed the more easily controlled brooks first and the grist mill became next in importance to the meeting house. Much as with the minister, the miller was granted land or some other advantage for building and maintaining the mill. Saw mills soon joined the grist mills, bark was ground for tanning; fulling mills were established and all primitive ways were employed to use the power available. Despite the flooding, the meadows provided hay to winter the cattle, pasture much of the year, and considering the fish to be obtained from it, the river was vital to the colonists continued existence.

Two fish stories of later years indicate the quantity that must have been available. In Stow, Captain Thomas Whitman passing near the river where Rams Horn Brook enters it, saw an almost solid mass of fish, and returned with his boys and four oxen to dip sixty bushels into his cart. A similar incident is told about a man passing across the fordway near Heart Pond in Chelmsford on Acton Street (Rte. No. 27). The brook was filled solid with shad and alewives and he filled his cart by scooping up the fish with his hands. This was near the end of the eighteenth century and another story told later, in 1880, by Captain Silas Tyler was as follows: — "The best haul of fish I ever knew was eleven hundred shad and eight or ten thousand alewives. This was in the Concord River just below the Middlesex Mills. Formerly there was what was called an island on the Belvidere side of the bridge near the mouth of the Concord. There were four fishing places, two above and two below the Concord River Bridge. Joe Tyler, my uncle, owned the two above and Josiah Fletcher those below the bridge . . . The law allowed us to fish two days a week in the Concord, and three in the Merrimack . . . People would come 15-20 miles on fishing days to procure these fish. Shad were worth $5 per hundred, salmon 10 cents per pound." Thus it is easy to understand how, in earlier days, the river directly provided food for anyone to take.

When the first towns were settled the river was not used for as many boundaries as you would expect. The towns were settled astride the rivers, and only later when they were divided was the easy boundary of the river used, and often this choice was the result of the great distance across the meadows from one piece of firm ground to another. The usual reason for the separation of the towns into smaller districts was that the people living in the more distant parts could not easily make the long trip to the required Sunday Meeting. The petition of the people of Carlisle when they first wanted to form a district separate from Concord is typical of all the others; "in order to their more convenient (sic) coming to ye publik worship of God, from which they are many times many of them hindred by ye Difficulty of passing ye river in time of flud and by ye great distance of their abode from ye place where ye publik worship of God is now upheld." Even today we can well understand the difficulty, although the fords used at first were soon replaced by bridges. Sometimes ferries were maintained by the town. For example in Sudbury, Thomas Noyes, in 1642, was "appointed to keep a ferry for one year, for which he was to have two pence for every single passenger, and if there be more to take two a piece."

Neither bridges nor ferries solved the crossing of the rivers, however, where there were meadows unless long causeways were built out from the high ground, and even to-day it is not unusual to have the causeways, that have been raised several times since, covered by water. High water too often washed the bridges away. Shattuck in 1835 writes "the first bridge was built across the Concord River from the point of land below Joseph Barrett's Esq. to Lee's Hill. In 1665 it was washed away, and another built the next year, where the present South Bridge stands.

Six or seven new bridges have since been built on the same spot." The expense of maintaining the bridges was sometimes a very controversial matter in town meeting, for as time went on and more people settled to the westward, the people who used the bridges most came from those outlying towns. To make sure that a town where an important inter-town bridge had been built, maintained it, the General Court had to direct that it be done and assess the other towns for part of the expense. The bridge Billerica built in 1657, at the Fordway was partly the responsibility of Chelmsford and Groton, and one year when they did not pay their share promptly, Billerica took up the planks. Carlisle paid part of the cost of keeping the North Bridge in Concord until they had the bridge to Bedford. This was a cooperative venture, each town agreeing to build a bridge to a pier in the middle of the river, but they could not agree on the place. Finally, Carlisle succeeded in having the bridge built where from their side they could approach the river on high ground, whereas Bedford had to build about a half mile of expensive causeway. East Sudbury was separated from Sudbury in 1780, and later (1835) took the name of Wayland. Here the meadows were especially wide and the newer towns to the west, dependent on them shared the bridges maintenance. Sudbury and Concord also had bridges on the Assabet. As settlement to the west increased Sudbury and Stow maintained what is now Russell Bridge in Maynard. Before this was built, in 1715, the people of Stow came all the way down to the North Bridge in Concord to go to Boston, although the bridge over the Assabet at West Concord was built before 1660. This route the people of Stow followed shows how the river influenced the direction of travel. In a similar way the road from Concord to Lowell was across the North Bridge and then followed the river to Chelmsford. The traveller to Wayland avoided crossing either river by going much as Route 126 goes to-day from Concord, and to Marlborough, after crossing the South Bridge one followed the southeast bank of the Assabet on what is now Old Marlborough Road out of Concord.

While, during the first century and a half of the occupancy of the valley by the English, the river influenced the people, the people did not influence the river much, but the advent of the factory system and its demand for power changed this, and about this time transportation on the river had a short revival. Previous to this time, it does not appear that the river was used much to transport anything, although it is said that those from Concord who settled in Chelmsford floated their goods down the river. This is believable and probably other trips of this kind were made but there is no record of them.

However, about the end of the 17th century a considerable increase in the use of the river for transportation took place due to the construction of the Middlesex Canal from Charlestown to Chelmsford crossing the Concord River at North Billerica, and using almost exclusively the water of the Concord River to flood its whole length. The canal was completed to the Merrimack in 1798, and a second grist mill and a second saw mill were erected at the dam in North Billerica. By 1803 the work was completed to Charlestown. The charter which had been granted in 1793 and extended in 1795, authorized the company to "render the waters of the Concord River boatable as far as Sudbury causeway and as much farther as the same can be usefully improved for that end and to open any canal, at any place in said County of Middlesex that may be necessary to connect said Concord River with the said Middlesex Canal".

Before discussing the effect this had on our river, we may mention, in passing, a prior canal between the Merrimack and Concord Rivers. Because shipments of lumber (rafts) had difficulty passing the Pawtucket Falls, "The Propriators of the Locks and Canals on Merrimack River" was incorporated in 1792, and succeeded in building by 1797 a canal from above the falls, 1½ miles, with four sets of locks to drop the 32 feet into the Concord River near its mouth. The traffic which this was built to carry from New Hampshire to Newburyport was soon diverted to Boston by the Middlesex Canal, but in 1823 this canal began a new function by providing power for the new cotton industry of Lowell.

In the meantime the transportation on the Concord River from Sudbury to Chelmsford or to Charlestown had begun, although at the beginning no effort was made by the Canal Company to improve the channel except that the improvement of the dam at North Billerica may have made the water a little deeper. The records seem to show that one of the principal reasons for the Canal Company's interest in making the Concord River 'boatable' was to transport iron ore to supply the several iron works at Chelmsford, but it is amazing to find so little recorded about commercial transportation on the river after the canal was operating in 1803. All mention of it is incidental to other matters. The History of the Town of Sudbury, listing mineral resources, refers to the excellent bog iron ore which was especially good for making cast iron. Dug from a swamp near Puffer's Pond, it was carted to Lee's Bridge and floated down the river to the forge at Chelmsford. In 1830 three hundred tons was thus transported. Shattuck in his History of Concord describing the Iron Works at West Concord which was finally abandoned says that "recently several tons were taken to Chelmsford by boat", and that would have been down the Assabet. He also says "boats frequently run from Boston through the Middlesex Canal and this river to this town and Sudbury". Some one of the past generation has told that the bricks of the Hildreth house on Lowell Road in Concord were brought up the Merrimack and Concord by boat from Haverhill, and the bank of the Assabet where they were unloaded can still be identfied by the broken pieces scattered about. The certainty of this is substantiated by chemical tests made for a former owner of the house who wanted to determine the source of the bricks.

There is also testimony before a legislative committee in 1860 which was investigating one of the many complaints of the farmers about the water on their meadows. John Sherman of Lincoln said: "I had a canal boat and used to clear wood from near my meadow, and boat it to the canal to Boston in 1816-17". "When we returned men had to draw the boat up. Couldn't get up the river with a load in dry weather. My boat drew something over 2 feet." Stedman Buttrick, who lived where he could watch the river from his window said; "I helped to clean out the bar for boats, full loaded with wood, could go down to the canal at Billerica." Hemen Ray of Lincoln said: "I boated on the Concord River, in 1816-17. We rowed from Bent's Landing down as far as Concord." Nathan Barrett who could watch from his house on Punkatasset Hill said; "There used to be a boat running, regularly, from here to Boston up to 1840. The bar was cleared out in 1835 to go through without grounding." Other evidence appears in the canal records which shows that "15 tons of coal made a sufficient load for those (boats) going up to Concord or Sudbury." And at a Lowell Historical Society meeting in 1874, John B. French of Billerica recollects "that on the Concord River there was a large business in summer by boats from Concord and other points on the river, transporting wood, goods, and lumber, and in floating rafts." Continuing he explained that ox cart was the only other way to move heavy goods in 1813-14. People rode horseback, and maybe the very fashionable had a chaise, but wagons had not appeared and the roads were not good enough for them. Dr. E. W. Emerson in writing of Ebenezer Rockwood Hoar, tells of a political speech he made " . . . on the occasion of the great political gathering of Whigs at Concord, in 1840, the campaign of Harrison and Tyler, when not only were the roads filled, but great numbers came on canal boats poled up from the Merrimack, and even from the Mystic by the Middlesex Canal. A bridge of these boats was made at the battleground . . . . " But it was not long before land transportation improved, and the railroads replaced the canal. Transportation on the canal ceased in the 1840's. Before its final death as a corporation, it tried to sell its property to the City of Boston which at that time had no water supply but wells and cisterns. Four eminent chemists testified to the quality of the Concord River water, and it could flow right down the canal from Billerica to the edge of the city.

Short though the life of the canal was, its authority to dam and use the Concord River water caused controversy for many years. The first dam at Billerica 1807 was promoted by the town to provide a grist mill. This was a leaky, unstable zig-zag barrier built across a chain of rocks which held up the water enough to increase the power available and channel the current to the sluice way for the mill wheel. The canal company purchased this but it was not enough to keep the canal full for its 22 miles to the Charles and 6 miles to the Merrimack, so the dam was raised and strengthened and this theoretically should do the job, for it made the mill pond 27 feet higher than the Merrimack above the falls and 107 feet above tidewater at Boston. It was not long, however, before it was discovered that sometimes the Concord had almost no current. (Only about one inch drop per mile for twenty-two miles) and to get enough water to operate in a dry summer the canal company took steps to clear out the channel by digging out the bars and mowing the weeds; and the farmers who had done this before cooperated as they wanted the water off their meadows in summer. The critical spots were a ledge of rock at the Fordway in Billerica about which nothing could be done, and Barrett's Bar near Punkatasset Hill in Concord, the Assabet Bar just below Egg Rock, Robbins Bar below Pantry Brook, and a few others all the way to Wayland which could be dug out and cleared of weeds. Mowing weeds might be a yearly job and although machines were devised to be pulled by oxen, (one man told of seeing 10-12 yoke working back and forth, almost completely submerged), it was often necessary for men to work with scythes, up to their necks in water. A new stone dam was built at Billerica in 1828 which helped some, but after the canal stopped operations and sold out to mill interests the demand for water was even greater.

To make matters worse, the City of Boston now decided they wanted a water supply and took Long Lake (now Cochituate) in Framingham, which provided about half the water in the Sudbury at the point where its outlet joined it. To avoid a threatened suit by the mill interests, the city built reservoirs at Whitehill Pond in Hopkinton, flooding 600 acres; and Fort Meadow in Marlborough flooding 300 acres (the latter on the Assabet) and actually provided a potential of more water than they took. The mills were delighted and seeing the possibilities offered to take over the maintenance of the reservoirs, and then pleased the city by purchasing them. Now they could store the water when the river was high and let it down during dry spells. And they did, but it kept the meadows from draining off so the farmer could get his hay and cranberries. The farmers complained again to the legislature but got no relief.

These mills which now exercised considerable control over the rivers were started on ancient sites which became very valuable privileges after 1800 when the application of power to the manufacture of yarn and cloth had become practicable. Hitherto, the power needed for grinding grain and sawing lumber was often obtained from the many brooks that were easily controlled. Only at North Billerica, Saxonville, and near the mouth of the river in what was then Chelmsford, was the attempt made to use the power of the river itself, and the dams were hardly more than baffles to channel the water. Many more sites were available on the Assabet Brooks than on those of the Sudbury and Concord, due to its narrow valley and nearby hills which provided a quick drop for the water. In Concord for example, there was only one mill on a brook tributary to the Sudbury or Concord, — the first mill of the settlement, while the three other sites were on Assabet brooks, — Temples on Spencer Brook, Wright's on Nashoba, at the outlet of Warners Pond, and Heywood's on Second Division Brook, the bottom of the fall being in each case about the level of the river.

The fact that the rivers could supply the new demand for power, substantially changed the character of much of the valley. Relatively large centers of manufacturing grew up along the banks. The site at North Billerica with an eleven foot drop became a worsted and woolen manufacturing village quite foreign to the staid old town. Below at East Chelmsford, later Lowell, a considerable development took place. Before 1800, River Meadow Brook coming out of Heart Pond in South Chelmsford through Carlisle and back into Chelmsford, had several mills and in 1807 it was extensively developed near its junction with the Concord by Moses Hale with a saw mill and a carding mill. Hale was very successful and then undertook to exploit the nearby river. At Wamesit where there was a 26 foot fall, he built a powder mill with forty pestles operating and producing a million pounds a year during the Mexican War. When he sold out, a man named Whipple improved the privilege, built a canal so that several mills could utilize the water, and a center of manufacturing was built up on the Concord River before the large Lowell Mills were even thought of. Two other sites nearer the Merrimack with 8 and 11 foot falls respectively were subsequently developed, and with Whipples formed a group independent of the large corporations that later got their power from the Merrimack and made the big and famous manufacturing center.

It was thirty-five miles up the river at Saxonville before another site on the Concord-Sudbury River could be found. The colonial grist mill there was superceded by a woolen mill in 1823 and began the manufacture of carpet yarns in 1837. The business continues to-day, the present occupant being the Roxbury Carpet Company. There was also a textile mill at the outlet of Long Pond which subsequently transferred its operation to the Assabet in Maynard. These were in Framingham and there were several other sites developed here during the early nineteenth century, but they are best described as in Ashland which was set off from Framingham, Hopkinton, and Southborough in 1846, after an intensive industrial development and substantial increase in population. This district had several small mills in the eighteenth century but it really boomed in the nineteenth. Cotton cloth, spool cotton, woolen mills, paper manufacturing, grist mills using grain brought by rail from the west, and finally the establishment of a great printing company which caused a boom in real estate. The bottom dropped out suddenly when the City of Boston, needing more water, received authority from the state to take the water of the Sudbury River, Farm Pond, and their affluents in 1872. The purchase of 600 acres of land for storage and the construction of dams to make three reservoirs holding nearly 5 million gallons proceeded and water that should have come down our rivers went to Chestnut Hill Reservoir in 1878. It spoiled the Ashland water powers and the town took years to recover. The mill owners were paid damages not only in Ashland but all the way to Lowell, for the water that they had lost, apparently forever. It was not forever, though for when, at Clinton, the Wachusett Reservoir was completed in 1898 less Sudbury water was retained, and after Quabbin came into use, none was needed for the city of Boston Water Supply. This storage at Ashland and Framingham did not affect the mills higher on the river at Southborough where there were good mill sites along the southern border of the town, and two mill villages grew up and operated worsted mills until recently.

Fortunately for the Concord River, the Assabet did not suffer as the Sudbury in losing its water. Only five miles up its course a cotton and woolen factory was built at Damondale in Concord, and a few miles farther a powder factory at the edge of Acton was built in 1835. The big development on the Assabet was at Maynard,—Assabet Village—part of Sudbury and Stow before 1871. The name had previously been Isabaeth, Elsabeth, Asibeth, or Elsibeth but in 1850 it was standardized as Assabet. It was not until 1846 that Amory Maynard and W. H. Knight, who had previously operated at Cochituate, purchased the land on which to develop this power. They were in time to get the Fort Meadow Reservoir that the City of Boston built, Boone Pond and other storage areas to insure a uniform supply of water. They were also in time to be well established to supply, during the Civil War, the demand for army blankets, a product on which these mills thrived for three more wars.

At Gleasondale, which is in Stow, the usual colonial mills were started before 1770. Fifty years later the dam was improved and a cotton mill erected, which as frequently happened, was later changed over to a worsted mill. Another town which was created by the power of the Assabet is Hudson, a part of Bolton and Marlborough before 1866. A mill for corn was there in 1700, and excellent power was available from the river and two brooks flowing into it. The village was first called Feltonville because of the distillery operated there up to 1812, making brandy from the many apples grown in the district. A worsted mill and a tannery then became the nucleus of the village which eventually became the center of the town of Hudson. Marlborough had now lost all of its Assabet River power to towns that had been set off from it, Hudson, below, and Northborough, above. By 1672 the latter had a saw mill near the center, and by 1846, four grist mills and five saw mills on its various brooks, and in 1814 a cotton factory on the river. Subsequently, dams at two other sites on the river powered small factories that still operate.

We cannot leave the Assabet without considering the two brooks which join it through Warner's Pond at West Concord. Together they drain the whole of Acton. The southernmost reaching out to Long Pond in Littleton and Fort Pond, from whence it gets its name, is joined by Heathen Brook out of the great Stow swamp and runs through South Acton to unite with the other, Nashoba Brook, just before entering Warner's Pond. It drops nearly 50 feet just after leaving South Acton, and the power was used to operate mills there. These as usual were first a grist mill, a saw mill, and a fulling mill, which later became one of the first efforts to manufacture woolen cloth in this country. The village before the coming of the railroad was called Faulkner's Mills. Other sites were later developed and a shoddy mill, a morocco factory, and a thriving piano stool factory continued there until recently.

The brook draining the northern part of Acton originates in several swamps in the south part of Westford. Called Nashoba it is joined near the junction of Route 2A and 27, by the outlet of Nagog Pond, fed by powerful springs. Although the drop at East Acton was not great, the flow of the stream was reliable, and on the site of Thomas Wheeler's early grist mill a more modern one was erected in 1840 by Daniel Weatherby, and the village there grew enough to have its separate Post Office. However, the western competition was too great and although the mill tried to continue by grinding mineral products it finally closed in 1910. Higher on the brook at Brook St. a pencil factory was started in 1848, which after a fire was reopened as a sash and blind factory, then as a print works, and finally ended in 1888 as a pencil factory again. The water rights at this site and at the small dam at the outlet of Nagog Pond were eventually part of the storage for Weatherby's Mills and Nagog was enlarged greatly beyond its natural size. It no longer contributes much to our rivers, as the Town of Concord took it for their water supply.

The control of the water by dams was not as serious for the river as the pollution caused by the mills. The great value of water power was often its convenience for washing impurities from the manufactured products, and these went down the river together with the chemicals used to dissolve them. The need to prevent pollution was recognized as early as 1663 in Marlborough. Within ten years of the settlement of the town, it voted: "It is ordered that no person shall lay or put any flax or hemp into any pond or brook within this town, where cattle use to drink, on penalty of paying to the town's use twenty shillings for every offense; and whosoever hath now any flax or hemp in any pond or brooke as aforesaid, shall cause the same to be taken out within four and twenty hours after the date hereof, on penalty of paying the said sum."

Dam and Gate House stand at Framingham's MDC reservoir.

A relic of a later war looks out over Hudson's Mill Pond.

At Northborough a railroad bridge crosses at the Woolen Mill Dam.

At Westborough is Piccadilli Brook, source of the Sudbury River. This old shoe factory reflects on a busier past.

An old stone bridge on the Sudbury stands on the boundary between Southborough and Hopkinton.

In Marlborough on the Assabet a trout fisherman wets a line.

Spring brings flood waters to the Assabet.

Swimmers take to the river at Fordway Bridge.

On the Concord River at North Billerica there is a dam

and two mills.

A young fisherman tries his luck.

The Concord at Billerica.

Duck boxes dot the marsh
at Great Meadows National Wild Life Refuge.

An aide at the Refuge paddles in from an inspection tour.

The cliffs above Fairhaven Bay at Concord overlook Lincoln.

NO *OTHER* mention of the pollution of the rivers appears for over 200 years. Then, in 1894, when the people of the valley thought the wet meadows was the cause of some cases of malaria, the General Court appropriated $20,000 to dredge the bars, remove the weeds, and do anything else that would "tend to the restoration of the marshes along the rivers to their original condition and to the abatement of malaria and other perils to the public health . . . " The owners of lands benefited agreed to share the expense, so it looks as if the farmers hoped to get their meadows again for hay. A survey showed that the river in summer at Farm Bridge in Wayland could not be expected to be over 19 inches higher than the water flowing over the flash boards at the North Billerica dam each morning. It was further shown that even if the dam were removed no appreciable lowering of the water would take place as the Fordway bar would hold it up. However, it was thought that by cutting channels through the principal bars, from Barrett's up, the water would be lowered about 5 inches at Concord and a few inches more gradually up to ten inches at Farm Bridge. Altogether 31,333.6 cubic yards of excavation was completed at various places over 14,075 feet along the river. This made the channel 5 feet over the 22 miles from the Fordway to Farm Bridge, and whatever else it accomplished, it made the canoeing much better.

The complaints about malaria continued, and in 1900 the State Board of Health was directed to investigate. This time refuse from factories was mentioned in the General Court's resolution. It was found that the City of Boston was taking all the Sudbury River water above Framingham, most of the year, except the 1,500,000 gallons per day they were oblig-ed to release and that this would continue until an-other source for Boston was available, and into this comparatively small amount of water released, there was discharged at Saxonville "a considerable quantity of water polluted in the processes of scouring wool and washing cloth, . . . rendering it very foul for a long distance below the village. In the drier portions of the year, this pollution is noticeable to the eye . . . six miles down the river."

The conditions on the Assabet were unbelievably worse, so unpleasant that no one any longer wished to go upon it. The report states that the most important of the sources of pollution are at Northborough, Hud-son, Stow, Maynard, Acton and Concord. Starting at Northborough "the sewage of about 400 mill opera-tives discharged directly into the stream; and the spent dyes and 5000 gpd of water used for washing cloth from the Northboro Woolen Co." In Hudson the river received the sewage from 18 business blocks including three hotels, 22,000 gpd of wool-scouring waste, 30,000 gpd of water used for washing hides in which process soap, lime water, and tan liquor are used; and the sewage from 700 employees in three shoe factories. At Gleasondale the sewage from 85 employees, but only 3000 gpd of waste. At Maynard, the waste from scouring 8,000-16,000 lbs. of wool a day, and the sewage of 950 employees. At Concord, sewage from 165 employees at the rubber company and 110,000 gpd of sewage from the Reformatory. Pressure was applied to correct these conditions, but it was many years before improvement was noticeable. After all the State was one of the worst offenders. Real improvement did not come until the woolen mills were out of business. Incidentally, it was decided that the malaria was due to the invasion of the towns by the soldiers returning from the Spanish War.

During the last half of the 19th century, the recreational use of the river and nearby valley increased extensively. There were fishermen—even some professionals—but their catch was mostly pickerel,—there were trappers, and large numbers of muskrat were taken, and the duck and snipe hunters obtained a good harvest from the meadows twice a year. However the actual number of individuals who participated in these activities was relatively small. Swimming was never a major activity due to the condition of the water. Only up to the first of July was the water reasonably free of weeds, and although there were a few swimming holes it could not compete with Walden for the local boys. Skating was very popular from early in the nineteenth century, and many who skated took the long trips to Billerica or Wayland. Boating increased tremendously and this brought many people to know the river intimately. In the days of Thoreau and Hawthorne, few boats were maintained, but in the last quarter of the century large numbers appeared to be used by people just to enjoy the outdoors. This can perhaps be attributed to the increasing number of people working in offices and factories—the first commuters. Improved types of boats were made, and by 1885 the river in Concord running parallel to Main St. was described by Bartlett in his "Concord Guide Book" as "very picturesque with its numerous landings at the foot of the gardens that slope down to the water, each with its little fleet of boats, dories, canoes, wherries, or other small outriggers." He says, "Every family has its boats, over seventy being kept between the old and new stone bridges, a distance of about two miles, and on a pleasant evening one is more likely to meet friends on the river than on the roads."

This was the "Golden Age" of the rivers, about 1870 to 1900, when the greatest number of people enjoyed them to the greatest extent. It was about this time that the general interest in Natural History had risen to a previously unexperienced height, and there was no place where it could be more easily and comfortably studied than the rivers. In the published diaries and letters of men who later became distinguished we can read of their sentimental almost worshipful attitude toward it. French, the sculptor and all his youthful friends had boats, and he well knew from every angle and in intimate detail the site for which his Minuteman was destined. He introduced his friend Will Brewster of Cambridge, later a famous ornithologist, and such was his love for the river that he acquired and preserved a large tract of land along its banks where he eventually spent most of his days. These two friends had a reunion on the river annually for many years, and although French had moved from Concord, he always returned for it, and the trip was never missed despite wind and rain which for others might seem to require a postponement.

The prophet of the river life, however, was George Bartlett. After he gave up business, he was the ever ready guide to any interested group of strangers, and always had spare equipment at his picturesque boathouse behind the Old Manse where he spent much of his time writing his Guide Book, magazine articles and poems about the river. He was the organizer of the "floats" and meetings for water sports that took place during the summer, on the Assabet, at Fairhaven Bay, or some popular picnic spot. These were well known and usually a place where the high land came out to the edge of the stream and frequently where a good spring of water could be found conveniently nearby. Concord became somewhat widely known as "Picnic Town" and in a Boston Transcript of 1870 we find:

> "If Queen Victoria should come
> And to that village go,
> She would not be allowed to sleep
> Till she had had a row.
> Next day a picnic they would make,
> Her presence would request,
> And up the river they would take
> Their much distinguished guest."

In addition to holiday breakfasts at Egg Rock, for which, one year, ninety tickets were sold, the principal annual observance took place early in the autumn at the same place. Under the direction of young Dan French, it was known as "Cornucopia" which was appropriate as there was always "Peace and Plenty" but there was probably a little joke tucked away in the name as the festival consisted mainly in a grand Corn Roast. Such was its fame that scores of guests from Boston and adjacent towns regularly made their appearance.

Requiring less preparation were the "Moonlight Floats", when on pleasant summer evenings, almost without pre-arrangement, boats would converge a short distance up from the mouth of the Assabet, and with the dories and larger boats in the middle, they would tie up to each other until the stream was filled from bank to bank several ranks deep. Then, led by the best voices an hour of singing was enjoyed as the float passed slowly down with the current.

One usually found George Bartlett among the leaders in the events on the river which accompanied the celebration of summer holidays elsewhere in Concord. Regularly on Fourth of July there would be boat and canoe races and other water sports in the afternoon and in the evening a "Carnival of Boats" with a hundred or more in line, some lighted with Chinese lanterns, some with transparencies representing the Old Bridge, the Liberty Bell, or the occupants costumed and posed in tableaux and lighted by colored fire. The bridges were all decorated and as the procession came to each, fireworks were set off. Along the banks the gardens of the houses were illuminated and filled with guests to a number difficult to credit. Imagine, if you can, that on July 4, 1879 (not a year of any particular significance), it was estimated that 8,000 people converged on Concord. The parade on the river ended at the North Bridge where a band played, and the sky was filled with fireworks.

At Bartlett's death in 1896, three hundred thirty-seven contributors placed a tablet in his memory at the "Hemlocks" on the Assabet, one of his favourite spots, and on it were inscribed lines from one of his poems.

Newspaper writers, not only in Boston but from across the country seemed to find the river a popular subject for feature stories. Each seems to have come to Concord to see the places of historic or literary interest and then gone home to write about the river.

Consequently people from other towns sought out the river and some came to settle, for at least part of the year, on its banks. In a Watertown weekly, August 25, 1886, a writer tells of his week at a camp on the west side of Fairhaven Bay, and his nearby explorations. He found on the northeast corner of the bay "Camp Solid Comfort", built in 1882 by four Watertown boys, who with their friends and relatives, kept open house through the season. Their guest book for the year showed 365 names. It apparently was appropriately named for one can still find there children, grand-children, and great-great-grandchildren of one of the boys. Farther up the river, a Newton camp and two Waltham camps amazed this writer by their substantial construction and comfortable surroundings. Near Sherman's Bridge, he writes "is a most hospitable camp, and on the Sunday the writer called, five carriages were there having brought twenty or more ladies and gentlemen to spend a beautiful day."

Back in Concord, near what was then the "Red Bridge" on Lowell Road was the Musquetaquid Boat House built in 1888 for four young men from Boston to spend their week ends and holidays from April to November, and to entertain guests from far and near who came by train, carriage, bicycle or boat. For their comfort they had bed rooms in the village but they got their meals at the boat house or at picnic spots on the river. They entertained their guests on the river, and were as proud of their craft as any yachtsman. The canoes in those days were as individual as yachts, and named "Flamingo, Cardinal, Eleanor, River Tramp, Towhattawan, Red Wing" and similarly. As these young men grew up and retired from business they continued their summer life on the river. It was their highway, — a short distance up the Assabet to their daily golf match, or on Sunday, a short paddle to Trinity Church on Elm Street.

Gradually the "Golden Age" ended, only its reflected glory extending into the twentieth century. It was a period of romance and sentiment best described, perhaps, by lines Bartlett quotes in one of his poems.

> "The boat is as full as a boat should be,
> Just nobody in it but you and me"

By the end of the century a canoe club was formed, and eventually built a commodious house on the river between the North Bridge and Monument Street, and people from Lexington organized the Lexington Canoe Club and built a house above the South Bridge. The Concord Canoe Club stated as a purpose of its organization: —"To keep control of certain points bordering on the river, to prevent their sale or use by objectionable people from camps, etc., and thus shut off Concord people from them." All of those who used the river hoped to preserve its natural surroundings, as many to-day plan to have it for future generations. In 1893, a letter to the editor of a local paper asks, "Do we need a Riverside Association? Why should we give so much time and attention to our roadsides and neglect our beautiful river? Coming generations will be glad to escape from our telephone haunted roads to the soul resting river, whose ways are ways of pleasantness, whose paths are paths of peace."

When the net work of trolley lines from the cities reached the river, about 1900, several boat liveries were established in Bedford and Billerica. These attracted many people, and becoming acquainted with the area they began to obtain small lots from the farmers along the river on which to build small camps.

Settlements grew to be densely populated in summer, and during the depression of the thirties, most of the places were occupied the year round and continued so thereafter, dominating the river in the lower reaches. A few isolated communities of a similar nature appeared in Wayland and Sudbury, but the breadth of the meadows made them less conspicuous. Unfortunately, the building boom of the fifties and the scarcity of land in Framingham, together with that town's lack of planning, enabled the developers to fill some of the low land near the river and build right up to the stream. In one place, a meander of 5000 feet—nearly a mile—was cut off by a channel of 360 feet which was made into more building lots. The whole district is especially susceptible to flooding at high water, and from this condition has arisen a demand that some measures of flood control be provided.

Before describing flood control measures established or projected, we may well consider the condition and problems of the river in 1950, which are extensively described in the 1950 report to the Sudbury Valley Commission. This was composed of the Commonwealth's Department of Agriculture, Conservation, and Health, and headed by the state planning board. The two major problems were sewerage and volume control to keep the river higher in dry seasons and lower in wet. Since 1900 there had been no official survey of the river but the Sudbury Valley Commission made a thorough investigation of all the aspects of the problems between the inhabitants and the rivers: —flood damage, pollution, drainage of agricultural land, maintenance of attractive recreational facilities, provision for mosquito control, wild life refuges, access by the public, reforestation of adjacent land, means to keep the river flowing in times of drought and the maintenance of the scenic beauty. The report emphasizes the difference of the Assabet from the Sudbury due to its greater and more uniform flow which allows it to pretty well clean itself of the impurities it receives, whereas the Sudbury with its nearly thirty miles of level river bed is still further debilitated by the retention of its water above Framingham. Regarding the Sudbury, the Commission made two definite recommendations: —(1) to connect Framingham and Natick to the South Metropolitan Sewerage System, and (2) to have the state acquire as much as possible of the land bordering the river in the meadow districts between Wayland and Billerica. The proposed diversion of the sewerage at once presented a problem, for sixty per cent of the flow of the river where the sewer waste joined it, would be lost, leaving in dry seasons only the meagre 1½ mgd released by the reservoirs, and most of this would be lost by evaporation before it reached the river's mouth. Consequently it was necessary to recommend an increase in the amount released from the reservoirs to 4 mgd just to keep the river flowing. But if this were done in a really dry season, it would draw down the reservoirs making them unsightly, unpleasant and perhaps unhealthy for the residents of the neighboring developments, so a problem remained. Possibly, it was suggested, that taking water from Cochituate as well as from the reservoirs would make the condition less noticeable but this shows the problem that has arisen due to the great increase in the density of population. As yet no dry season has been experienced so the problem has not had to be faced.

One point emphasized in the report was the value of the meadows as a safety valve in the time of severe floods. Without the meadows to absorb the excess water, the damage caused by the freshet of 1936, and the hurricanes of 1938 and following years, would have been much greater than it was. Before any action was taken in regard to flood control as a result of this report, federal legislation following Hurricane Diane in 1955 made it possible for another agency to concern itself with the rivers.

The Federal Congress in 1956 passed legislation authorizing the Soil Conservation Service of the Department of Agriculture to administer an act for Watershed Protection and Flood Prevention. As a result of damage caused by Diane it was possible to take advantage of the provisions of this act, and an association of landowners, called Conservation Districts was formed in Middlesex and Worcester Counties, to cooperate with the state and federal governments, for the improvement of the SuAsCo watershed. A survey shows that at this time the watershed consists of 11% cities, towns and roads; 2% cropland, 18% grassland, 4% lakes and streams, and 65% woodland. The plan proposed (1) land treatment by farmers and landowners, (planting, ditching, terracing, and the like) (2) eight floodwater retarding structures on the Assabet tributaries, and (3) drawdown and release rates on six reservoirs on the headwaters of the Sudbury. As of November 1961 one of the eight structures has been started. This project is primarily to prevent excessive flood damage from unusual storms, and is not concerned with releasing water in dry seasons; and is only of little value to the cause of wild life production and protection.

Fortunately other volunteer groups have appeared to try to preserve the natural beauties of the river and as much of the adjacent area as possible in the cause of conservation. An example of what can be done was shown by a resident of Concord in acquiring pieces of the Great Meadows below Concord, and turning them over in one large parcel to the Federal Fish and Wildlife Service for a Waterfowl Refuge. A later and much more extensive project was started in 1952 by a group of public minded citizens who believed that "open spaces"—including brooks, rivers, ponds, marshes, and swamps — are a vital human resource and that the values which attract people to the country in the first place, can be preserved during the process of urbanization. The Sudbury Valley Trustees, Inc. was formed, which in addition to acquiring and preserving whatever lowlands they could, marshalled aid in 1961 to obtain government action to acquire the principal marshes of the Concord and Sudbury Rivers, 8000 acres in all, by the Bureau of Sports Fisheries, the Department of Natural Resources, and local communities.

In addition, since authorized in 1957, many towns have established municipal Conservation Commissions charged generally with the development and protection of their natural and watershed resources. Besides these the towns of Lincoln and Concord have formed organizations similar to the Sudbury Valley Trustees to work toward the same objects, with perhaps more elasticity than the municipal organizations. These are local instruments which will work to preserve the river borders even beyond the limits originally envisaged. The success of these projects seems assured, and the movement shows signs of spreading over the whole valley. It therefore may be expected that the appearance of the river and its surroundings along a considerable length of its course may continue as we know it, at least from a distance. Near to, the picture is not so encouraging. Nowhere has the nuisance of outboard motor-boats been solved. Also, the river is not yet nor soon will be clean enough for bathing. Improvements must be made in many municipal sewerage systems that still discharge their waste into the streams. Even now the chemicals used to treat this waste, and the waste itself, continue to affect the vegetation in the river. The detergents used tend to neutralize the naturally acid water which has caused the disappearance of the white water lilies which once lined the borders of the streams. Also this neutral or slightly alkaline water seems to be ideal for a tiny plant commonly called Duckweed which covers the surface of the river in summer and thrives on the fertilizer of the nitrates from the filter beds. Many years will pass before the towns along the rivers will find other ways to treat their waste, which is increasing daily, and only an enlightened public can bring this about and keep the gains that have been made.

That is the picture of the rivers today, over much of their course, beautiful streams, worth keeping, with several groups organized to try to prevent further deterioration, and to do what they can for improvement of conditions through their own efforts and by educating the public so that the various levels of political bodies concerned will cooperate.

DISTANCES ON THE CONCORD RIVER

IN MILES

	from Billerica Dam	*from Egg Rock Concord*
Fordway Bar	.23	11.16
Turnpike Bridge	3.09	8.30
Carlisle Bridge	6.55	4.84
Barrett's Bar	10.07	1.32
North Bridge	10.69	
Red Bridge	11.24	
Assabet Bar	11.39	0.00
Elm St. Bridge	12.23	.84
South Bridge	12.34	
Heath's Bridge	13.86	2.47
Fairhaven Bay	15.53	4.14
Lee's Bridge	16.14	4.75
Gulf Brook	17.44	6.05
Sherman's Bridge	18.63	7.24
Canal Bridge	21.46	
Bridle Point Bridge	22.53	
Saddle Rock and Farm Bridge	22.98	11.59
Dam at Saxonville	29.12	17.70
Warner's Pond Brook	14.20	2.81
Damon's Pond	15.93	4.54

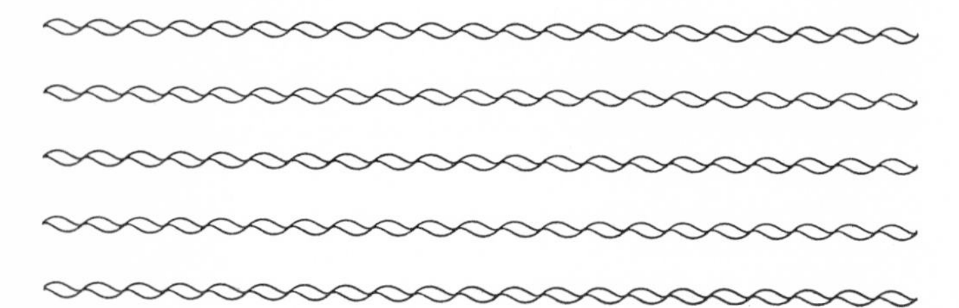

Printing:	*Text, Barre Publishers*
	Illustrations, The Meriden Gravure Company
Design:	*Shirley Errickson*

Cover:	*The Assabet River at Concord*
Endpapers:	*Concord Bridge*

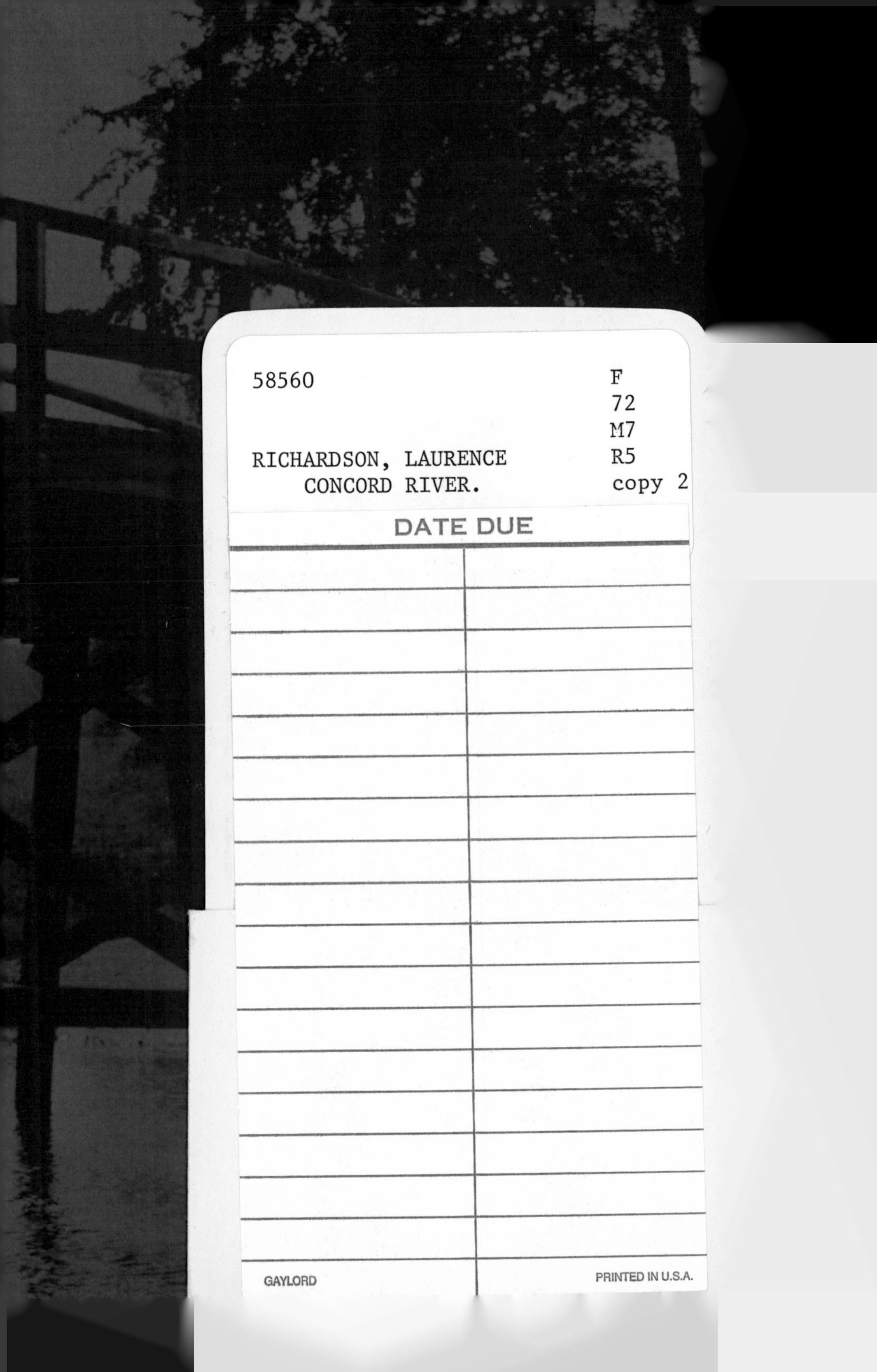